HORSE GUNNERS

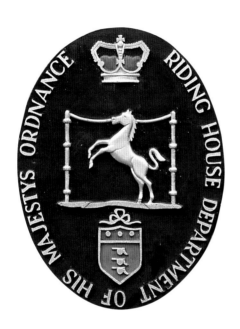

Horse Gunners

A pictorial record of
The King's Troop Royal Horse Artillery

Edited by Major W.G.Clarke (Retd)
with photography by
Julian Calder and Henry Dallal

ISBN 0-9520762-8-4 hardback
ISBN 0-9520762-9-2 softback
ISBN 0-9520762-5-X special edition

Published by
The King's Troop Royal Horse Artillery
Ordnance Hill, St. John's Wood, London NW8 6PT, England

Publishing consultant: Barbara Cooper
Editor: Maj W G Clarke (Retd)

Photographs: Julian Calder/Henry Dallal/Darren Gray/Sean Lewis
Design: Alan Hamp
Production: N G Hemsley
Colour reproduction by Reed Digital, Ipswich, England
Typeset in Sabon

Contents

Officer Royal Horse Artillery
 c 1793.

Foreword
by The Duke of Richmond and Gordon

THE ABIDING INTERESTS of my ancestor, Charles, 3rd Duke of Richmond, were defence and horses. It was therefore appropriate that he should be involved in the development of the first substantial horse-drawn gun in England. As Master-General of the Ordnance, the Duke automatically had overall responsibility for the two Troops of Horse Artillery which were created by Royal Warrant early in 1793. He liked the idea of the new gun so much that he decided to take a more personal interest, summoning the 'A' Troop to Goodwood so that he could train it himself. The horses were housed alongside his hunters in the magnificent classical stables which had been built by Sir William Chambers some thirty years earlier. The men and their horses were trained here on the Sussex Downs, where hunting and private horse-racing already took place. The guns were parked in front of the house, and it is said that my ancestor did a great deal to create the Troop's fighting spirit.

The Duke had also always been very interested in science and engineering: many of his books in the library testify to his fascination for contraptions. He must have enjoyed becoming involved in the development of the new six-pounder gun. Two more Troops were founded before the end of the year. Despite his obvious fascination with the mounted artillery, it must have been very difficult for the Duke that Britain was at war with France, as he was of recent French descent, and even Duke of Aubigny, where he owned two châteaux. I often wonder if exiled members of the French aristocracy came to stay here at Goodwood in the 1790s. Whatever the case, the Duke clearly enjoyed immersing himself in the practicalities of the Horse Artillery. He ceased being Master of the Ordnance in 1795, but only seven years later reached the apotheosis of his equestrian passion by founding Goodwood racecourse on the top of the hill.

Richmond

Introduction

Horse Gunners is a pictorial record of a typical year in the life of the King's Troop. Divided into seasons and with the activities of each month separated out, this book seeks to impart to the reader a flavour of the culture and history of a unit that is unique among the regiments of the British Army. Whether it is the more mundane routine of life in the capital during the winter months, or the excitement and adventure that is enjoyed during the show season, each photograph has its own story to tell.

The officers and soldiers who serve in the King's Troop are, of course, part of Britain's modern army and are trained as such. The ceremonial role that they carry out, however, is drawn directly from the past: indeed, from a period when all horse artillery batteries were so dressed and equipped. We must be grateful therefore to His Late Majesty King George VI for instigating the formation of the Riding Troop in 1946, and for his generosity when visiting St. John's Wood the following year, in granting the title the 'King's Troop'.

For those who live in London, the King's Troop will no doubt be familiar for its appearances on State occasions. For the vast majority of people throughout the country who have witnessed the famous Musical Drive, the name will conjure up galloping hooves, speeding gun carriages, jingling harness and dashing horsemanship. This book, as well as capturing the splendour and excitement of public occasions, has another purpose. It goes behind the scenes and shows the day-to-day effort, dedication and skills of many different kinds that are required to produce the excellence towards which the Troop is constantly aspiring.

I hope that Horse Gunners, as well as giving pleasure, will add to the respect and pride with which the King's Troop is regarded by so many.

S.R.HALL

Major
Commanding,
The King's Troop Royal Horse Artillery

Detail from 'I' Troop at Fuentes d'Onoro; see page 12.

Origins

THE KING'S TROOP ROYAL HORSE ARTILLERY is the Saluting Battery of Her Majesty's Household Troops. It was formed in 1946 at the express wish of his late Majesty King George VI to revive the peacetime practice of Royal Salutes fired in Hyde Park by an RHA Battery dressed and equipped in the traditional manner. Today the King's Troop is the only horsed battery in existence in the British Army. It is responsible not only for the firing of Royal Salutes in Hyde Park, but also for representing the Royal Regiment of Artillery at all the 'great ceremonies of State' that take place in the capital and at Windsor each year.

Anyone watching the Troop gallop into action in Hyde Park, dismount at the canter, unhook and bring their guns into action in a matter of seconds, might be forgiven for thinking that the whole performance had been perfected purely for ceremonial reasons, or to impress the tourists. On the contrary, these drills are echoes of a display of battlefield techniques once vital to the waging of war. Indeed, the King's Troop is the guardian of a heritage that has survived virtually intact since before Waterloo.

The first two troops of horse artillery were formed at Woolwich on 1 February 1793. They came into being as a result of the long perceived need to provide an artillery arm capable of rapid manoeuvre. By continental standards the British had arrived rather late at the idea of a highly mobile, self-contained artillery arm. As early as 1759 Frederick the Great of Prussia had devised and introduced the first truly mobile form of horse artillery which he called *Reitende Artillerie*. With teams of light 6-pounder guns each drawn by six horses, in pairs, with the drivers riding postillion on the near side and gunners mounted behind on their own horses, Frederick's brain-child became the model for the rest of Europe.

The man most instrumental in the formation of the Royal Horse Artillery and who might be called the father or at least the godfather of the Regiment was Charles, third Duke of Richmond and Lennox, who was Master General of the Ordnance from 1782 to 1795. The post in those days was a civilian, political appointment conferring a seat in the Cabinet. At the time, the army was organised on the extraordinary system by which the artillery and engineers did not come under the Secretary at War, but under the Master General of the Ordnance. The Lennoxes were a splendidly eccentric and unpredictable family, and when they perceived some goal they were apt to pursue it with great vigour.

It is said that the Master General was converted to the horse artillery idea by an incident in which an enterprising young officer of the Royal Artillery was ordered to send some guns from Winchester to Southampton to quell a riot. Using his initiative he requisitioned two post-chaise teams, hitched a 6-pounder behind each, packed as many gunners as could be squashed in to more post-chaises, and sent the whole lot off at the gallop. Legend or myth, what is certainly true is that the personal interest of the Duke of Richmond and the encouragement he gave to the project ensured its success.

Such was the Duke's enthusiasm for this new arm that shortly after the first two Troops were formed, 'A' Troop, it is said, was summoned to Goodwood, the family's country seat so that the structure and training of the Troop could take place under the Duke's own close attention. The new horse artillery Troops were described at the time as 'the most complete thing in the army' and very few changes took place in their organisation up to 1813. The officers and men for this new corps were selected from the Royal Regiment as a whole, earning their place within the Troops according to their conduct and professionalism as officers and soldiers.

Since commissions in the Royal Artillery could be obtained only by successfully completing the courses at the Royal Military Academy, Woolwich, it is hardly surprising that the RHA, with its selection system, should have distinguished itself so brilliantly in battle during the early years of its existence. Their first notable successes were marked at Ross and Vinegar Hill in Ireland during the rebellion of 1798, as well as their conduct during the ill-fated Corunna campaign with Sir John Moore in 1808-1809. It was however, during Wellington's Peninsular campaign from 1810 until 1813 that the reputation of the RHA Troops was firmly forged. Altogether five Troops took part. Although none arrived in time to take part in earlier battles – such as Talavera – horse artillery was represented at virtually every action thereafter.

Of the many battles in which the horse artillery were involved it was perhaps the conduct of Norman Ramsey, second captain to Robert Bull, commanding elements of 'I' Troop at Fuentes d'Onoro on 5 May 1811 which best epitomises the panache and professionalism of the RHA Troops of the period. This action was later described by Sir William Napier thus: 'The mass (of French horsemen) was rent asunder and Norman Ramsay burst forth sword in hand at the head of his battery, his horses breathing fire, stretched like greyhounds along the plain, the guns bounding behind them like things of no weight, and the mounted gunners followed close, with heads bent low and pointed weapons, in desperate career'

By the time of Waterloo in 1815 the RHA Troops had increased from the original two of February 1793 to a total of fourteen, and their reputation as a 'corps d'élite' among the regiments of the British Army was widely accepted. Of these, eight were to take the field of battle with Wellington's army on 18 June.

Much has been written on the events that took place during the battle. It is sufficient to relate here the two principal actions for which their commanders subsequently became famous. The first concerns the action of Bull's Troop with their heavy 5½ inch brass howitzers in support of the Guards at Hougemont Farm early in the battle. Here they were called upon to direct fire over the heads of their own troops on to the enemy in the wood nearby. The result was extremely effective and accurate fire with shrapnel. Within ten minutes, much to the satisfaction of the Duke of Wellington and Colonel Frazer, the Commander Royal Artillery, the wood had been cleared of French tirailleurs.

The other more conventional action was that of Mercer's Troop when summoned to assist in repelling a French cavalry attack at the centre of the allied line. As they descended the reverse slopes towards the main position amid the roar of cannon and musketry, Mercer observed through the smoke the leading squadrons of enemy cavalry moving toward them at a brisk trot. Mercer immediately ordered the line to be formed for action. The order 'case shot' rang out and the leading gun was unlimbered and began firing almost as soon as the word was given. The first blast from the guns reduced the French to a walk, and subsequent rounds of shot decimated their ranks. Disobeying a previously issued order from the Duke that the gunners must take refuge at such times in the infantry squares, Mercer stayed where he was, continuing with his detachments to spray the front of the French positions with a rhythmic, withering fire until the enemy were piled high in front of the gun line. At last the French commander cried 'La Garde récule' and the slaughter was ended. For Mercer and his troop the moment and this part of the battle were won.

After the conclusion of the campaign against Napoleon there ensued a long period of peace in Europe, and for the next forty years the British Army was involved in nothing more exciting than the mundane tasks of garrison duties. During this period it was allowed to run down and stagnate. At home the soldiers existed on 1lb of bread and 3¼ lb of beef a day, were badly housed, and were dressed in uniforms that were elaborate but unsuited to anything other than parades. In addition they lacked the training and expertise that had prevailed at the time of Waterloo. All these factors were to have a telling effect upon the performance of the Army when the monotony of garrison duties was broken in 1854 with outbreak of war in the Crimea.

Horse artillery participation in the Crimea was comparatively small, given that there were two brigades of cavalry involved. Initially there were only 'C', 'I' (which at the time was the 'Rocket Troop' and later became 'O') and a 'Ball Cartridge Brigade', an organisation that was later in the campaign to be reformed as a

Left: 'I' Troop at Fuentes d'Onoro, 5 May 1811.

Right: Royal Horse Artillery - 1854, possibly at Woolwich.

Below: Lt Grylls and Charger, 'C' Troop RHA, Crimea 1854.

horse artillery troop and retitled 'B'. Later, in 1855, these would be joined by 'A' Troop from England.

The RHA Troops saw action at most of the great battles of the campaign but it was Balaclava and the ill-fated charge by the Light Brigade for which 'C' Troop and the Light Brigade are most famous. Prior to its involvement with the Light Brigade, 'C' Troop, under the command of Major John Brandling, had just returned from an all night picket duty at Inkerman and was about to water and feed the horses and take breakfast with what little rations there were, when they were ordered to move immediately to the assistance of the Heavy Brigade. Abandoning all thoughts of breakfast or refreshments of any kind, the Troop set off on its task.

After a hard ride along rough tracks to the escarpment the Troop came into action on the right rear of the British cavalry. Once hand-to-hand fighting with sabres had taken place and the Russians were attempting to reorganise themselves, Brandling brought 'C' Troop's deadly guns into the affair. At a range of half a mile he fired 49 rounds of shot and case into the Russian cavalry. The effect was devastating. After only a few

minutes the Russians broke and fled, incapable of any further effort that day.

No sooner had the Troop completed the action than it was ordered once more to assist the cavalry. On this occasion it was to be the Light Brigade and its charge against the Russian guns in the north valley. 'C' Troop however, was by now almost spent; the horses were tired and worn out from their previous exertions; there was little hope of them following the cavalry down the valley. Subsequently they were left behind as the Light Brigade galloped off to their deaths.

A few years after the campaign in the Crimea, three horse artillery batteries, 'D', 'E' and 'F' (better known today as 'E', 'D' and 'G') were despatched to India to assist in the final operations to quell the mutiny that had begun the previous year. As a result of the mutiny, control of India by the East India Company was abolished on 1 November 1858. For the Royal Artillery it meant the absorption in 1861 of the magnificent European troops of horse artillery into the Royal Horse Artillery. These troops, from the Bengal, Madras and Bombay presidencies, took their place as lettered batteries in the RHA brigades of the time.

Both 'Royal' and ex-Company batteries continued to serve on and to distinguish themselves in India and Afghanistan during the latter part of the 19th century. The service of Gunners in India during this century could provide enough material for a book on its own but unfortunately there is place here for only one of the most celebrated RHA actions of the time by 'E/B' at Maiwand. This battle, which took place on 27 July 1880, was the climax to a mismanaged and ill-advised operation in the Second Afghan War. A small force consisting of the 66th Foot (2nd Battalion the Berkshire Regiment), 'E' Battery 'B' Brigade RHA, with two Indian battalions and two Indian cavalry regiments,

'Saving the Guns': 'E' Battery 'B' Brigade RHA at the Battle of Maiwand. Second Afghan War, 27 July 1880.

The Chestnut team of 'E' Battery RHA, 1897. Believed to be the first known photograph of a RHA team without anyone riding on the limber.

Senior non-commissioned officers of 'P Battery RHA. 1899.

were challenged by a large and well-armed Afghan force complete with modern artillery.

During the ensuing battle the guns of 'E/B' proved inferior to those of the Afghans, resulting in heavy casualties amongst the battery. Ultimately, as a result of a breach in the ranks of one of the native battalions by the Afghans, the gun position of the 'E/B' RHA was overrun. In this mêlée two guns were lost and many horses killed. Fortunately due to the great heroism shown by so many in the battery that day, four guns and the majority of the men were saved and made their way back to Kandahar with the remainder of the British force. Two VCs were awarded for the action: Sergeant Mullane and Gunner Collis. The battery is now in suspended animation as 145 (Maiwand) Battery Royal Artillery.

The British Army's last campaign of the 19th century was the South African or 'Boer' War of 1899–1902 in which a total of ten RHA batteries served. Most fought throughout as normal gun batteries equipped with the 12-pounder field gun. Some, however, such as 'J' Battery, were converted during the campaign to become 'Mounted Rifles'. Many gallant actions were fought by units of the Royal Artillery during this war. Of particular note is that of 'Q' Battery RHA at Sanna's Post. Here they displayed stoic resistance as they continued to man their guns in open country with no available cover, against withering and accurate fire from Boer riflemen. For their gallantry four members of the battery were awarded the Victoria Cross, including the Battery Commander, Major Phipps-Hornby RHA.

Whilst the war in South Africa occupied much of the British Army, another expedition – this time an international brigade, was sent to China to assist in putting down the 'Boxer' rebellion. Among those who took part were 'B' Battery RHA, who were sent directly from England. By the end of 1902 both campaigns were over. The lessons learned in South Africa were to have far-reaching effects upon military style and practices in the years leading up to the First World War in 1914.

At the outbreak of war on 14 August 1914 there were more than twenty regular RHA batteries in existence. By the end of hostilities in 1918 the number had increased to twenty-seven. Horse artillery batteries served in virtually every theatre of operations, from the Western Front in France and Flanders to Gallipolli and Mesopotamia. Indeed, it was a 13-pounder of 'E' Battery RHA that fired the first artillery round of the war on 22 August 1914 near Bray in France.

For the RHA the most famous action of the war took place at Néry on 1 September 1914 when 'L' Battery, in support of 1st Cavalry Brigade, were surprised in the open by a German cavalry division. During the subsequent action all but one of the Battery's guns were destroyed. The Battery Captain, the Battery Sergeant Major, and the Number One kept this gun in action for over an hour against immense odds; they were all later awarded the Victoria Cross.

The end of the Great War in November 1918 also brought about an end of an era for the British Army. Horsed cavalry and, with it, the horse-drawn artillery were, it was said, obsolete. Although it was to take some years before the change from horses to mechanical 'horse power' was complete, it was obvious to everyone

'L' Battery RHA. The last gun in action. Néry, 1 September 1914.

'A' Battery The Chestnut Troop, with Light Dragon tracked gun tower and 3.7" howitzer. Aldershot 1938.

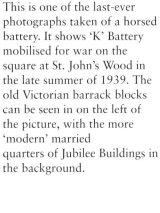

Right: 'K' Battery RHA 1939. This is one of the last-ever photographs taken of a horsed battery. It shows 'K' Battery mobilised for war on the square at St. John's Wood in the late summer of 1939. The old Victorian barrack blocks can be seen in on the left of the picture, with the more 'modern' married quarters of Jubilee Buildings in the background.

Left 'K' Battery firing the last Royal Salute before the SecondWorld War, August 1939.

Right: An 18/20 pounder and Dragon gun tower of 2 RHA at the Belgian frontier, May 1940.

that change was inevitable. The great Defence Review of 1922 brought many other changes to the post-war Army, in particular its size and structure, as it shrank once more to peacetime proportions.

On completion of the review in 1924 there remained just fifteen batteries in the RHA order of battle. For the British Army life between the two world wars was an endless round of garrison duties interspersed with tours of duty overseas. At home RHA batteries and brigades were invariably stationed in places such as Aldershot, Newport, Trowbridge and St. John's Wood. Overseas, there was one brigade in Egypt and four batteries with cavalry brigades in India.

Mechanisation of the RHA began in 1934 when 'A' Battery (The Chestnut Troop) and 'M' Battery exchanged their horses and 13-pounders for the 3.7inch howitzer towed by a Light Dragon gun tower. By the outbreak of war in 1939 every battery and brigade had been mechanised except 'K', who were at St. John's Wood as the saluting battery of His Majesty's Household Troops. 'K' were mobilised as a mounted battery in September 1939, but fortunately were not required to take their faithful animals into the maelstrom of war and by Christmas the horses had been returned to the Remount Depot. 'K' were subsequently mechanised along with 'G' Battery (Mercer's Troop) at Wotton-under-Edge in Gloucestershire to form the new 5 Regiment RHA.

During the Second World War RHA batteries and regiments served in virtually every theatre of operations. In 1940 1, 2 and 5 Regiments RHA were involved in the battle to save France and Belgium after the 'Blitzkrieg' unleashed upon them by German forces. As resistance in France collapsed all three regiments were eventually evacuated from either Dunkirk or St. Valery, except for 'B/O' Battery of 1 Regiment, who were unfortunately taken prisoner when St. Valery was captured.

As the battle for Europe raged in France and the Low Countries, 3 Regiment and the newly formed 4 RHA experienced their first taste of action in the Western Desert in June 1940 when the Italians declared war on Britain and her Empire. By 1941 the Italian army had been reinforced by the German 'Afrika Korps' commanded by General Erwin Rommel. With the arrival of German troops the fortunes of the British 8th Army changed dramatically, as the Germans surrounded the garrison of Tobruk and pushed the British back towards the Egyptian border. It was during one of the many battles and actions to relieve Tobruk that the RHA won their first VC of the War.

2Lt Ward Gunn of 'J' Battery RHA was in command of a Troop of 2-pounder anti-tank guns attached to the Rifle Brigade when it was attacked by more than sixty German tanks. Throughout the engagement Gunn moved about his guns encouraging the crews and reorganising them as casualties mounted and guns were destroyed. After some time there was only one gun left in action and Gunn and the Number One operated this, all the other members of the crew having been killed or injured. Before long the fire of several tanks was concentrated on the loan active gun until it, too, was silenced with a direct hit and Ward Gunn was killed. Gunn's posthumous VC was the only one awarded to a British Gunner actually serving the guns during the Second World War. For this gallant and remarkable feat of heroism during the battle, in 1954 'J' Battery were granted the honour title 'Sidi Rezegh'.

By 1943 there were five RHA Regiments serving in the North African campaign, and a new 6 Regiment RHA was serving at home in the United Kingdom. After taking part in the early battles of the Italian campaign, 3, 4 and 5 Regiments were sent home to the United Kingdom to prepare for Operation Overlord, the invasion of Europe. 1 and 2 Regiments RHA remained in Italy until the end of hostilities in 1945. After the war there was the usual reorganisation and reduction of the armed forces and within Gunner circles there was considerable discussion as to whether the RHA system was still required within the Royal Regiment. Did the Regiment need this 'Corps d'élite' and, if so, what role should it adopt?

After much deliberation and several attempts at reorganising the RHA to adopt other disciplines, it was decided that five regiments should remain, all in the field role and where possible, in support of armoured formations. Some have since lost their RHA status as the Army and the Royal Regiment have been reduced and reorganised over the years and others have adopted new disciplines – such as the airborne role of 7 Regiment. There are currently three RHA regiments in existence – two in the United Kingdom and one in Germany. Additionally there is the King's Troop RHA at the old battery station of St. John's Wood in London, which serves to remind us all of the standards, traditions and heritage of the Royal Horse Artillery in the marvellous days when all were horsed.

Above: A 2-pounder anti-tank gun of 3 RHA mounted 'Portee' style, in action in the Western Desert, 1941.

Below: The guns and tanks of 3 and 5 RHA lead the parade of British troops during the Allied Victory Parade, Berlin 1945.

Enter The King's Troop

THE ROOTS OF THE KING'S TROOP are to be found in the history of the 'Riding House Department of His Majesty's Ordnance' formed by Royal Warrant on 1 January 1803. The first Riding Master of this new organisation was Captain C.A. Quist, an elderly German officer from Hanover, whose appointment came about at the express wish of King George III. It has been said that the cavalry of the King's German Legion largely influenced the horsemanship for which the Royal Horse Artillery became renowned. This is not surprising, for although the British were in many ways behind the continental armies, they were not too proud to learn or to borrow.

Captain Quist was a student of the Spanish Riding School of Vienna and brought many of the continental methods of training horses and riders with him. He was particularly well known for working horses between the pillars as practised in Vienna, and the Troop's own crest bears the same figure of a horse between two pillars as that used by the Spanish Riding School today. Initially,

the Riding Troop was borne on the strength of the Corps of Royal Artillery Drivers, but later it was established as an independent unit within the Horse Brigade. In 1857 the Troop, along with the rest of the Royal Regiment, ceased be commanded by the Master General of the Ordnance and was brought under control of the War Office. Captain Quist continued to command the Troop as the Superintendent until his death in 1821 at the grand age of ninety-one years. His horse 'Wonder' died at the age of forty and was subsequently buried at Woolwich. On the demolition of the original Riding Troop stables at Woolwich in 1969 his gravestone and that of other much loved and distinguished chargers were moved to St. John's Wood Barracks, where they remain to this day.

The first Riding Master was posted to the Troop in 1858 and in 1873 a Major Superintendent replaced the rank of Captain Superintendent. This splendid old rank lasted until 1947 when it was decreed that the Troop, being a horsed battery rather than a training

Captain C. A. Quist, first Superintendent and Riding Master to the Riding House Establishment, 1803. This painting, which hangs in the Officers' Mess at St. John's Wood, depicts Quist with his remarkable horse *Wonder*, who lived until he was 40. His gravestone, along with those of other famous chargers, stands only 30 yards away fom the Mess, by the manège.

Students on the jumping lane at the Army Equitation School, Weedon between the two world wars.

establishment, should have a Commanding Officer in command rather than a Superintendent. In the early days of its existence the Troop was primarily concerned with the improvement of horsemanship within the Regiment and for the training of officers' chargers. It was also responsible for the equitation training of the Gentlemen Cadets at the Royal Military Academy, colloquially known as the 'Shop'.

In 1903 the Riding Troop returned to the RHA fold after a short period on the establishment of the Royal Artillery. It was at this time that its numbers were increased and the Troop took on the task of the training of officers and NCOs of all branches of equitation. During the First World War personnel from the Riding Troop were very busy training hundreds of officers for Kitchener's New Army Divisions. To cope with this increased workload a reserve training brigade was created at the unoccupied St. John's Wood Barracks in 1915. They also requisitioned part of the cricket ground at Lords, using much of the sacred turf as manèges and the pavilion as accommodation for course personnel.

One of the Troop's other duties was to provide trained horses for use by senior officers of the Regiment, the Army Council and occasionally foreign attachés and Dominion representatives. Indeed, when His Majesty King George V visited Woolwich in 1918 the Troop also supplied the Sovereign's Escort. With the creation in 1919 of a new riding establishment at Weedon, the Riding Troop RHA was divided into two parts. One half remained at Woolwich and the other, under the command of Lieutenant-Colonel Jack Livingstone-Learmonth, moved to Weedon where Major C. T. (Taffy) Walwyn gathered about him a strong group of Riding Masters and senior NCO instructors in order to get the new organisation off to a flying start.

The first course started the same year with a syllabus very similar to that used until very recently by the Long Military Equitation Course at Melton Mowbray. On joining the course students were issued with an unbroken 'remount', a half-trained animal (last season's remount) and a fully trained horse. Each student rode his trained horse twice a day and his half-trained and remount once. During the week, periods of riding were interspersed with lectures, demonstrations, visits, farriery, veterinary work and fencing in the gymnasium. Apart from the latter, much else is still taught at Melton Mowbray.

One other feature of the course was the emphasis placed on hunting. Weedon was in the centre of excellent hunting country surrounded by such famous packs as the Pytchley, Grafton and Warwickshire. Officers hunted two days a week which, it was believed, developed 'an eye for the country and tested their reactions in difficult circumstances'. The chase across open country undoubtedly gives the rider a more secure seat in the saddle and, of course, a better understanding of his horse's ability. These values remain as relevant today as they did in the halcyon period between the wars.

During the great review and reorganisation of the Army in 1922, the Cavalry Riding School, which had been established at Netheravon immediately after the First World War, moved to join the Gunner Riding Establishment at Weedon and to form the Army School of Equitation. The Riding Troop at Woolwich remained in existence carrying out the same duties as before, until it was finally disbanded on the outbreak of the Second World War in September 1939. At this time also the last of the horsed batteries, 'K' RHA, stationed at St. John's Wood Barracks as the saluting battery, was also mechanised. Not long afterwards the officers and men of 'K' moved to Wotton-under-Edge in Gloucestershire to form the nucleus of the new 5 Regiment Royal Horse Artillery.

In late 1945 the people of Britain were anxious to repair the ravages of war and to return as quickly as possible to the normality of peace. The King was also keen to see the life of the capital return to normal, with the resumption once again of as many of the traditional State ceremonies as could be organised and achieved after six long years. One of the ceremonies that he wished to be resumed was the firing of Royal Salutes on royal birthdays and State occasions by a Royal Horse Artillery battery 'dressed and equipped in the traditional manner'.

In due course a letter from the King's Principal Private Secretary arrived at the Headquarters Royal Artillery, expressing the King's wishes on the matter and concluding that he expected the new battery to perform its first salute on the next anniversary of his birthday – 13 June 1946. In the austere winter of 1945 the task of finding sufficiently experienced men, the right type of horses and of course some horse-drawn guns for the new Troop, was a daunting prospect.

In the event, officers, NCOs and men with pre-war experience were drawn from virtually every corner of the Regiment and assembled at the temporary base of Horseshoe Barracks, Shoeburyness, where the only available artillery stables existed. Draught horses used for drawing the carts that collected spent shells from the mud flats were pressed into service with the Troop. They were joined by horses of almost every age and background from various Remount Depots around the country. By May 1946 the new Riding Troop Royal Horse Artillery, now in an advanced state of training for its first ceremonial duty, moved with 59 horses and 110 officers and men back to the old barracks at St. John's Wood. Here they replaced the London District Signal Troop that had occupied the barracks throughout the war. Once the Troop was 'home' again at the Wood, work continued in earnest to prepare for the impending Royal Salute. Whilst training progressed, the barracks were returned to their original use. The manège once again became a manège and the riding school ceased to be a gymnasium. With the floor returned to tan, the school resounded once again to the sound of horses and men undergoing equitation instruction.

For the salute in June 1946 the Troop used 18-pounder guns, as sufficient 13-pounders had not yet been assembled for use. Being short of the full battery complement of horses, the detachments rode on the limbers and the Troop went in and out of action at the walk. The first post-war Salute was fired without a hitch at noon on 13 June 1946. The King was well pleased, as indeed was everyone at the Wood. After much hard work and against great odds, a magnificent job had been done by all ranks and this would set the seal for the future.

From this hurried beginning the Troop progressed rapidly. Soon more horses were obtained and 13-pounder guns replaced the heavier 18-pounders. The winter of 1946 was spent in serious training for the famous Musical Drive of pre-war days, and the first performance by the gun teams of the new Riding Troop RHA took place at Aldershot in the summer of 1947.

This photograph of the Riding Troop formed up at St. John's Wood Barracks for the first post-war Salute on 13 June 1946, clearly shows the old horse lines on the edge of the square, with the riding school in the background and the Officers' Mess lawn (now gone) in the top right-hand corner. The guns were 18-pounders, as enough 13-pounders could not be found. Because of a shortage of horses, two men from each detachment rode on the limbers.

His Majesty King George VI with officers of the Troop during his visit on 24 October 1947.

Below: One of the Wood's most prized possessions: the document written by Major (then Lieutenant) Eddie Boylan, on which The King made his alteration to the Troop's name.

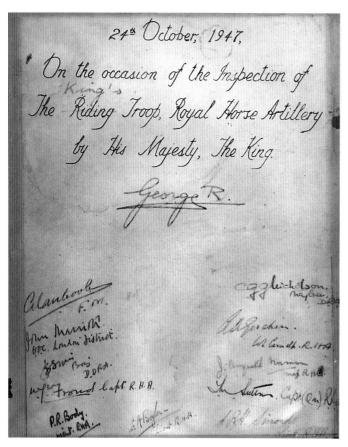

On 24 October 1947 King George VI visited the Troop at St. John's Wood Barracks. Although the pre-war Riding Troop had been inspected on several occasions by a reigning monarch, this was the first occasion when St. John's Wood had been privileged to host such a visit. For the King's inspection the Troop were mounted in full dress on the Parade Square. Later, whilst enjoying pre-lunch drinks in the Officer's Mess, the King electrified everyone around him when he said "I believe you would like to be called the King's Battery?" The Superintendent at the time, Major J.A. Norman, asked rather daringly if it could be the 'King's Troop' to which His Majesty agreed with the words "All right, so long as it is mine I don't mind what you call it".

Later, when signing the visitor's book, he crossed out the word 'Riding' and inserted 'King's'. On her accession to the throne, Her Majesty Queen Elizabeth II decreed that the title should remain during her reign as a tribute to her father, who was so instrumental in its creation.

Until 1951 the King's Troop was retained on the strength of the Royal Artillery as a normal operational battery, but with ceremonial duties. From this year onward the operational commitment became simply the supply of reinforcements to other units as and when they were needed. In 1949 the introduction of National Service brought a rich mixture of recruits to the Troop. Not surprisingly perhaps, many came from the world of National Hunt racing, including some who were to find fame later in life in the world of show jumping. There were others however, some even from the ranks of professional football, such as Cliff Jones, the Tottenham Hotspur and Welsh international footballer, who spent a rigorous but happy two years as a gunner at St. John's Wood.

Apart from the bonus of receiving so many recruits with considerable experience in horsemanship there was also the effect they had upon the Troop sports teams, for the jockeys came with a good deal of boxing ability, learned from many a bout in the annual stable boys boxing competitions. This proved quite useful for the London District boxing tournaments, despite the disadvantage in height and reach when matched against the Guards!

On Wednesday 6 February 1952 came the news that His Majesty King George VI had died quietly in his sleep. To the Troop fell perhaps its saddest duty when, on Monday 11 February 1952, they provided a gun carriage to carry the body of the King from Sandringham to Wolverton Station on the first part of its journey to London. On arrival at King's Cross, the King's coffin was placed upon a gun carriage drawn by 'F' Sub-section, the 'Blacks', to the Lying-in-State ceremony at Westminster Hall. This period of national mourning culminated on 15 February with the State

The coffin of His late Majesty King George VI passes into the Strand on its way to Westminster Hall, 11 February 1952.

A detachment of the King's Troop passes under Admiralty Arch during the Coronation procession, 2 June 1953.

Picket Mounting on the Parade Square at St. John's Wood during the 1950s.

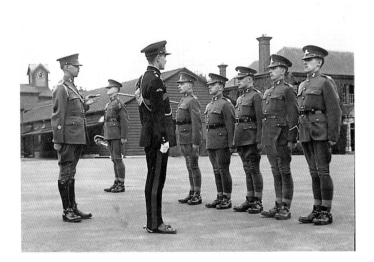

Coronation procession through the streets of London. The life and culture of the King's Troop during the 1950s differed little from that of a pre-war horsed battery. Indeed, the service dress uniform worn for guards, duties and routine parades, was virtually the same as that worn by the British Army prior to the Second World War. In mounted Service Dress knee puttees were still the norm: 'single puttees' for routine mounted parades and rides and 'double puttees' for Stable Picket and 'best wear'. The latter were exactly as described – twice the length of the former! Rolling them on to one's legs at the correct interval was a skill that required much practice.

Funeral, during which the Troop fired the minute guns – 56 rounds, one for each year of the King's life. This was repeated later that day at Windsor when the coffin was taken from the railway station to St. George's Chapel.

After the sadness of the previous year there came the jubilation of the new Queen's Coronation on 2 June 1953. As one would expect, the Troop was heavily involved in these celebrations: firing the traditional Royal Salute to mark the occasion and taking part in the

The '50s were also the decade during which the King's Troop consolidated its reputation as the premier equestrian display at both military tattoos and civilian horse shows throughout the country. Indeed, the first show of each year then, as it is now, was the Royal Windsor Horse Show with Her Majesty the Queen very often in attendance for the Saturday night performance. Other regular displays during the show season included the Royal Tournament, the armed forces own show at Earls Court, as well as many of the county agricultural shows up and down the country. The reputation of the Troop was also enhanced by the achievements in the world of Three-Day Eventing by the Commanding

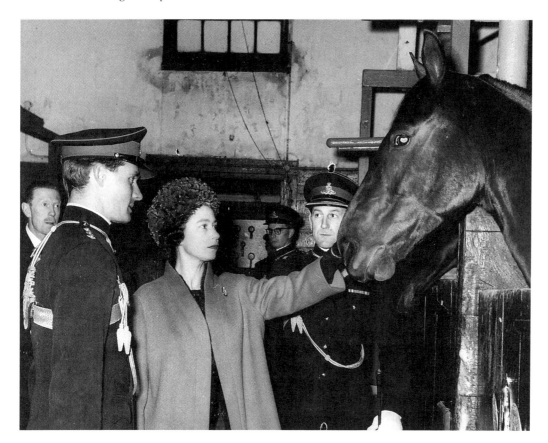

Captain James Templer introduces his horse *M'Lord Connolly*, with which he won the European three day event championship, to HM the Queen during her visit to the King's Troop, November 1962.

Officer, Major (later Lieutenant Colonel) Frank Weldon. With his great horse *Kilbarry* Major Weldon was part of the Gold Medal winning team at the Melbourne Olympics in 1956. The contribution of Troop officers to this sport has since become almost legendary. After Weldon came Colonel Bill Lithgow as *Chef d'Equipe*, as well as Captain (later Major-General) James Templer, a member of the British team at Tokyo in 1964. More recently, during the past two decades, two other Commanding Officers, Major Malcolm Wallace and Major Charlie Lane have both performed the duties of *Chef d' Equipe* for the British team.

In 1957 the Troop took part in the making of the Royal Artillery recruiting film 'Right of the Line' when they re-enacted the action of 84 Battery RFA in 1918. During the great German offensive that was designed to end the war in six weeks, the battery found itself trapped behind enemy lines with only one way of escape – a headlong gallop in full view of the enemy, hurdling fallen trees in the process. The shooting for this dramatic scene took place on the range area near Long Valley, Aldershot, with the Troop dressed in First World War uniforms complete with steel helmets and drawing 18-pounder guns. The act of hurdling fallen pine trees with gun teams at the gallop broke several wheels during rehearsals, so it was decided to place ramps in front of the trees, out of sight of the camera shot, in order to complete the film without further mishap. The result was

a most marvellous example of teamwork and discipline that both the survivors of 84 Battery and those of the Troop who took part must have been very proud.

By the early 1960s the King's Troop, along with the rest of the Army, bade farewell to its National Servicemen and welcomed the new 'Regulars': the first of many changes that were to affect both the Troop and the Army during this radical decade. The changes were never more obvious than during the very first visit of Her Majesty the Queen to the Troop at St. John's Wood on 15 November 1962. Here the Troop were on parade in each of the Section Lines, in the 'new' No 2 Service Dress (Mounted Order) complete with jack boots. Within a year the ancient style of jack boot which had been worn with full dress since the 19th century was replaced by the 'butcher' or polo-style boot now commonly worn with all forms of mounted dress.

In 1964 the Troop travelled abroad for the first time in its history when it took part in the British Military Tattoo, held during a British Trade Week in Copenhagen. This visit caused great excitement in the Troop for many reasons, not least of all the challenge of embarking the horses on to aircraft at Gatwick Airport. After much deliberation it was decided to walk the horses up a long narrow ramp into the aircraft – a DC6. To everyone's surprise (and the Veterinary Officer's relief) the horses loaded without much fuss and emerged at the end of the

The King's Troop providing
sound effects for the *1812
Overture* during the British
Tattoo in Copenhagen, 1964.

Firing the Minute Guns for the
State funeral of Sir Winston
Churchill, St. James's Park,
February 1965.

The King's Troop in action at the end of the Musical Drive and Display at Royal Windsor Horse Show.

Below: Walking the horses to Regent's Park during the equine 'flu epidemic, April 1965.

flight as if they had just stepped off the Troop horsebox! So successful was the show in promoting British products abroad that the whole process was repeated the following year in Milan. 1964 was also the year of the Tokyo Olympics at which the Troop provided two members of the Three-Day Event team – Sergeant Ben Jones, the Troop Equitation Sergeant, who rode *Master Bernard*, and Captain James Templer with *M'Lord Connolly*. Captain Templer had in fact left the Troop the year before having been Centre Section Commander for three years.

The following year the Troop took part in one of the greatest ceremonies of State when the nation bade farewell to its wartime leader, Sir Winston Churchill, with a full State Funeral in London. As was customary on these occasions, the gun carriage was drawn by ratings of the Royal Navy. Because Sir Winston had reached the great age of ninety years at his death, the duty of firing the minute guns, one for every year of his life, was divided between the King's Troop, who fired the first sixty rounds and the Honourable Artillery Company, who fired the remainder.

1965 was also the year in which the British equestrian world was struck down with a particularly virulent strain of equine flu. There were no shows at all during the early part of the season and from April to June all Royal Salutes were carried out at the walk. Morning exercise entailed leading the horses on foot to and from Regent's Park where they also enjoyed some excellent and for them, unfamiliar, grazing! Other notable events during the 1960s included the parade in May 1966 at Horse Guards to commemorate the 250th anniversary of the formation of the Royal Artillery, the State Visit and Royal Review for King Faisal of Saudi Arabia in May 1967 and the visit to Canada later that year for 'Expo 67' – The World Festival in Montreal.

This time the horses were transported in the more modern Boeing 707 jet-engined freighters for the transatlantic flight from Gatwick. A total of 27 horses were carried, three abreast, in these remarkable aircraft and as before, the Troop 'hairies' took it all in their stride. The site of 'Expo 67' was on a newly created island in the centre of the St. Lawrence River. The Troop performed the 'Earls Court' Musical Drive as part of an 'equestrian spectacular', in a marvellous new stadium, L'Autostade, that seated more than 25,000 people. Using a well-tried formula from previous shows, the Drive culminated with the gun detachments marching on at

Unloading the horses at Montreal Airport for 'Expo 67', September 1967.

S/Sgt Ben Jones with the British Three-Day Event Team shortly after being presented with the Team Gold Medal, Mexico 1968.

the end of the display to bring the guns into action firing two rounds of Troop fire – all of which received a rapturous welcome from the Canadian hosts.

The following year saw S/Sgt Ben Jones once again selected to represent Britain, in the Three-Day Event at the Mexico Olympics. His mount, *The Poacher*, was specially loaned to him for the Games. The story surrounding the vital part played by Ben Jones in this Gold Medal winning team during atrocious weather conditions is legendary and on return from Mexico he was treated to a marvellous welcome by all ranks of the Troop at a special reception in the Barracks.

In September 1969 after years of planning and discussion, the King's Troop finally moved from St. John's Wood to Combermere Barracks, Windsor, the home of the Household Cavalry armoured regiment, whilst the long overdue demolition and rebuild of the ancient barracks took place. For many who had served in the old Victorian barracks with its wooden stables and spartan accommodation, this was a very sad day. It had its own unique atmosphere; indeed, on summer days there was very much an air of bucolic serenity about the place, broken only at certain intervals by the clatter of hooves and the staccato sounds of the Orderly Trumpeter.

Although the Troop had moved to Windsor, the married families remained at St. John's Wood, most living in Jubilee Buildings, the married quarters block at the rear of the barracks: which entailed daily commuting for the married soldiers. For the firing of Royal Salutes and other State ceremonial events the Troop were allowed the use of Regent's Park Barracks where, on the day of each ceremonial event they arrived from Windsor very early in the morning. During this difficult period the Troop continued with the usual round of ceremonial duties as well as travelling, far and wide, including, for the first time in their history, a visit to the British Berlin Tattoo in 1971.

After two and a half long years at Windsor the Troop marched back into the new St. John's Wood Barracks on 17 April 1972. Two months later, on 6 June, Her Majesty the Queen paid the Troop a great honour when she visited the new barracks. There were many other notable events during the 70s. Among the more important being the inclusion of the Troop in the march past Her Majesty at Buckingham Palace at the end of the Queen's Birthday Parade in June 1973 and later in August the provision of the Queen's Life Guard. These additions to the ceremonial calendar once again brought great changes to the life and culture of everyone at the Wood.

In June 1977 Her Majesty the Queen celebrated her Silver Jubilee and among the many festivities was a great ceremonial parade and march through the streets of London. The Troop, as usual, played a prominent part in the proceedings, leading the Sovereign's Escort and State Coach from the Mall to St. Paul's Cathedral. Later that year the social and working life of the country was plunged into chaos with a national fireman's strike. For several months during the autumn and winter of that year St. John's Wood barracks became a military fire station, and most of the Troop personnel were employed on fire-fighting duties. Fortunately, after a few months everything was resolved and Troop life returned to normality. As part of the Army's reorganisation during the 70s the Troop were given a new operational role: that of forming two Home Defence Companies in time of war. Work on this extra role had to be fitted into the normal training year and from 1980, 'mobilisation training' became a fixed item in the winter training season.

1982 was a year of great contrasts in the history of the King's Troop. During the summer months there was national outrage and revulsion as a result of the terrorist bomb attacks by the IRA on the Household Cavalry in Hyde Park and the Band of the Royal Green Jackets, a little closer to home, in Regent's Park. These incidents brought about yet more changes to the way the Troop carried out its business, with tighter security and anti-terrorist measures that changed well-worn routines and practices. On a brighter note, later that year, elements of the Troop crossed the Atlantic for the first time since 1967, to perform a shortened version of the Musical Drive, at the World Horse Spectacular in Atlantic City.

The annual routine of Troop life during the 1980s continued in much the same way as it had for the past twenty or more years. The year was split into Section and Troop training periods during the winter and spring, and the show season almost always began with the Royal Windsor Horse Show. In 1987 there was also a full Royal Review in Windsor Great Park to celebrate the Troop's 40th anniversary. The annual show season continued to include many old favourites although by now there were fewer each year. The Troop managed several more trips abroad including once again, the Berlin Tattoo. Change, however, was in the air. Transport costs had increased dramatically over the years, and this, added to other organisational costs, meant that many of the agricultural shows that had been regular venues in the past could no longer afford the complete Musical Drive and Display. The Troop adjusted to these new demands by developing several short two and four gun displays.

With the reduction and reorganisation of the Army in the early 1990s came yet more change. By the middle of the decade Government legislation dictated a policy of

The funeral of Diana, Princess of Wales, September 1997. The cortège passes into Whitehall on its way to Westminster Abbey.

equal opportunities across a wide spectrum of employments and this included the Army. Consequently, the Troop admitted women to its ranks from 1996. In 1997 the Troop celebrated its Golden Jubilee with a Royal Review in Regent's Park on Cumberland Green, the exact spot that had been used for the very first post-war Review of the Troop in 1964. Later that year the Troop took a central role in one of the most moving events to be seen in the United Kingdom for more than a generation. On 31 August 1997 Diana, Princess of Wales was killed in a road traffic accident in Paris: an event which provoked one of the greatest outpourings of national and international grief ever known. At her funeral on 6 September, the King's Troop provided the traditional gun carriage and team of black horses for the procession from Kensington Palace to Westminster Abbey.

The close of the 20th Century brought with it the end of perhaps the oldest and most famous military show ever staged – the Royal Tournament. The final performance took place on 31 July 1999, bringing to an end 109 years of military pageantry and professionalism. The King's Troop had performed the Musical Drive at this show every year since the late 1940s, at both Olympia and, from 1951, at the Earls Court Exhibition Centre. Indeed, the 'Earls Court Drive' was the basis of every other Drive and Display that the Troop performed over the years.

The new millennium brought further challenges and events. For one year only there was the Army 2000 show on Horse Guards Parade. Apart from performing the ever-popular Musical Drive, the Troop also provided soldiers as 'extras' for other historical scenes such as the charge of the Union Brigade at the battle of Waterloo in 1815. By far the most important event for the Troop in recent times however, took place in April 2002 when they were called upon to provide the gun carriage for the funeral and Lying-in-State of Her Majesty Queen Elizabeth the Queen Mother. She had passed away quietly at Windsor on Saturday 30 March, little more than 50 years after the death of her husband King George V1. To mark the occasion on Monday 1 April, Royal Salutes were fired at every saluting station in the United Kingdom. The Lying-in-State began on Friday 5 April when Her Majesty's coffin, borne upon a gun carriage of the King's Troop, began its mournful journey from the Queen's Chapel at St. James's Palace. Thence it proceeded in sombre procession along the Mall to Horse Guards Parade. Once through the archway of London District Headquarters the cortège proceeded down Whitehall to Westminster Hall.

During the period of Lying-in-State at Westminster Hall, officers from the King's Troop were called upon to assist with the duty of guarding the catafalque. This is a unique honour and one that had never before been performed by officers from the King's Troop. The final duty came on Tuesday 9 April when Her Majesty was once again borne upon the same gun carriage that had carried her husband fifty years earlier from Westminster Hall the short distance to Westminster Abbey for the funeral service.

Today, the King's Troop remains firmly established at St. John's Wood Barracks and continues with its primary task as the saluting battery of Her Majesty's Household Troops. Despite the vicissitudes and vagaries of time and change, the 'raison d'être' of the Troop remains the same as it has ever been: to maintain the standards and traditions of the Royal Horse Artillery in all 'the great ceremonies of State' and, if possible, to improve upon them.

JANUARY

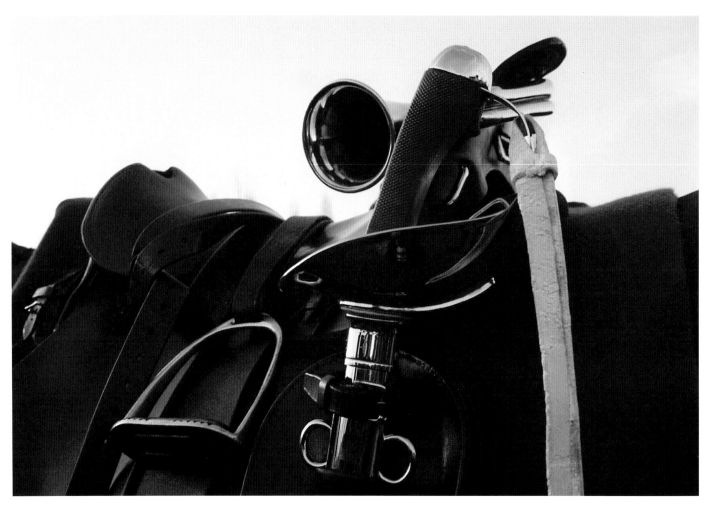

THE DAWN OF THE NEW YEAR at St. John's Wood invariably begins with half the Troop enjoying the final few days of well-earned leave. By the middle of the month all have returned and the serious business of the annual training cycle resumes. At this time of year the training programme is as varied as it is interesting. There are, of course, the usual draught parades for salute rehearsals, as well as the training of young horses and soldiers. This phase is known as 'section training'. In addition there is the inevitable period of 'mobilisation training' to ensure that standard military skills are kept up to scratch. While all this activity is going on other soldiers are fortunate enough to be involved with the winter training of horses at Melton Mowbray and the race training of others at both St. John's Wood and Larkhill.

A fine close-up study of a trumpeter's accoutrements: saddle, sword and bugle.

Previous page: A gun team en route to Wormwood Scrubs training ground to take part in the first salute rehearsal of the year.

Right: In 'column of route' the Troop negotiates the busy London traffic on its way to Wormwood Scrubs training ground.

The training ground at Wormwood Scrubs resounds to the rattle of gun wheels and harness, as the teams go through their paces during the Section Training period in late January.

A welcome break for both horses and men during training for the Musical Drive at Wormwood Scrubs.

A picture of concentration by both drivers and their horses as they begin the first draught training period of the New Year at Wormwood Scrubs.

The end of January brings the first salute rehearsal of the year and a welcome change to the training programme at Old Oak Common.

FEBRUARY

BEFORE THE ANNUAL period of section training is in full swing, the Troop prepares itself for the first ceremonial occasion of the year: the Royal Salute on 6 February to mark the Queen's Accession to the throne. The format for the salute is the same as most others – a gallop into action in Hyde Park. Mid-winter however can sometimes bring problems of its own: deep snow or hard frost, for example, will prevent the usual gallop down the Park, and on these occasions the Troop usually walk or trot into action. Once the salute is over the Troop returns to the cycle of Section Training and, for some, participation in such winter equestrian pursuits as hunting, point-to-point and the annual Royal Artillery race meeting at Sandown Park.

Royal Salute
FIRED BY
THE KINGS TROOP
ROYAL HORSE ARTILLERY
ON THE OCCASION
OF
ANNIVERSARY OF H.M. THE QUEEN'S
ACCESSION TO THE THRONE

Previous page: A fine view of the Troop as they gallop out of action on 6 February having fired a Royal Salute to commemorate the 50th anniversary of the Queen's accession to the throne.

Opposite: A sparse crowd of onlookers at the saluting base in Hyde Park is a clear indication that even the spectacle of a Royal Salute is not enough to tempt the tourists out of their warm hotel rooms on this crisp morning in February.

Resplendent in greatcoat order with the red plumes of the Royal Artillery atop their busbies, the Royal Artillery State Band provides the music for the Troop as it gallops into and out of action at all Royal Salutes.

This page: At Sandown Races.

Opposite: Tailors at work, and a full rehearsal for the Annual Administrative Parade at Old Oak Common, Wormwood Scrubs.

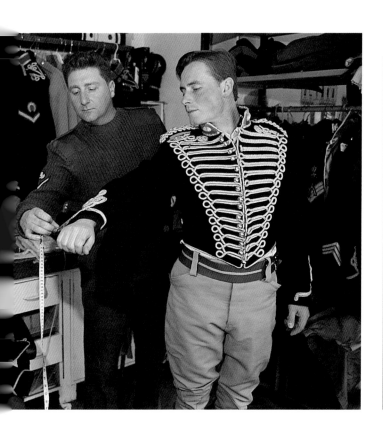

MARCH

MARCH WINDS bite into the heavy serge material of the army greatcoats as the gun-teams begin the serious business of collective Troop training at Old Oak Common on the open fields at Wormwood Scrubs, West London. The Troop routine now consists of twice-weekly draught parades; training horses and soldiers for both ceremonial duties as well as participation in the famous Musical Drive. The King's Troop Musical Drive and Display has been performed on many occasions overseas, as well as at countless agricultural and military shows throughout the United Kingdom. The training is rigorous, as one might expect, but it is equally enjoyable for both horses and soldiers, as can be seen in many of the photographs in this book.

Previous page: The General Officer Commanding London District and his staff arrive at the parade ground at Old Oak Common to review the King's Troop during their annual administrative parade.

Preparations for the annual administrative inspection begin with many hours spent cleaning leather and steel at St. John's Wood, as well as carrying out the inevitable and lengthy rehearsals at Wormwood Scrubs.

Before the GOC's parade there is a Full Dress Rehearsal at which the Director Royal Artillery is the Inspecting Officer. Afterwards, the Director invariably pays an informal visit to the various departments at the Wood, as can be seen in the following photographs.

On the occasion of the visit of

Her Royal Highness The Princess Royal

Anne

On 28ᵗʰ March 2002

During the very busy month of March, the Troop was honoured by a visit to the Wood by HRH The Princess Royal.

On the occasion of
The Administrative Inspection of
The King's Troop Royal Horse Artillery
By
Major General C R Watt CBE
General Officer Commanding London District

On 26ᵗʰ March 2002

On the occasion of the visit of

Brigadier C C Brown CBE ADC

Director Royal Artillery

On 20th March 2002

APRIL

APRIL SHOWERS are something that the Troop hopes will not dampen the Annual Administrative Inspection, which usually takes place in Regent's Park during the second week of April. This spectacular parade, with the elegant classical terraces of Cumberland Green in the background, resembles in almost every way the great military reviews of the 19th Century. The most important ceremonial occasion during the month, however, is the Royal Salute to mark the Queen's Birthday on 21 April. Much of the rest of the month is taken up with Troop training as the drivers and gun detachments hone their skills to perfection during countless days of practice at Wormwood Scrubs training area. By the end of the month the officers and soldiers of the King's Troop are ready for the challenge of yet another busy summer show season.

Previous page: A sub-section coming out of action at the Training Ground during the annual administrative inspection.

Very occasionally, on the death of a senior member of the Royal Family, or a distinguished soldier or statesman perhaps, the King's Troop is called upon to perform the saddest of its duties. On pages 60 to 63 are pictures taken at the funeral of Her Late Majesty Queen Elizabeth The Queen Mother.

On the day of the funeral itself, the King's Troop performs the traditional duty of firing the minute guns: generally one round for every year of the life of the deceased. On the occasion of the Queen Mother's funeral the minute guns were fired from Green Park.

MAY

MAY IS THE MONTH of the Royal Windsor Horse Show, which has been part of the Troop show calendar for more than fifty years. In 2002 the show took on a completely different format to celebrate Her Majesty The Queen's Golden Jubilee and became a grand display entitled *All the Queen's Horses*. Once again the Troop were centre stage with the famous Musical Drive for each performance of this spectacular show. In addition to the display, members of the Troop competed in all the main show jumping and skill-at-arms competitions, often with great success. Other activities of note during the month include participation in the annual Aldershot Military Show. Interspersed with all these events there is, of course, the continual routine of training for ceremonial duties.

Previous page: The King's Troop march past The Queen at the beginning of the Musical Drive and Display at the Royal Windsor Horse Show.

Following pages: Pictures of the Troop taken at Windsor, during *All The Queen's Horses*, showing various aspects of the Musical Drive.

After the glamour and excitement of Royal Windsor comes the down-to-earth business of more training at Wormwood Scrubs in preparation for the next important event.

JUNE

GLORIOUS JUNE: probably the busiest month in the ceremonial calendar of the King's Troop, which always begins with a Royal Salute to commemorate the Coronation of Her Majesty the Queen on 2 June 1953. This occasion is quickly followed by Royal Salutes to mark the Queen's Birthday Parade at Horse Guards (at which the Troop also ranks past Her Majesty) and, on 10 June, the birthday of His Royal Highness the Duke of Edinburgh. For the Golden Jubilee year of 2002 there was also the grand march and procession through the streets of London.

By the middle of the month the business of State ceremonial is usually left behind and the Troop embarks on its annual travels around the United Kingdom to perform the Musical Drive. In addition, some individuals are lucky enough to compete in the various military show-jumping competitions held at Melton Mowbray at this time.

Previous page: The King's Troop march past at the head of Her Majesty's Household Troops during the Queen's Birthday Parade.

Opposite: Scenes from the early morning rehearsals for the parade at Horse Guards.

Before taking part in the march past Her Majesty The Queen on Horse Guards Parade, the Troop fire a 41-gun salute in Green Park.

Above: On Horse Guard's Parade the Household Cavalry salute the guns of the King's Troop as they march past.

Left: A fine study of the Section Commanders as they march past the Royal Dais in perfect line.

For the Queen's Golden Jubilee Parade through London, the Troop provided two sections. One section is pictured here with the Gold State Coach and the escort of the Household Cavalry Regiment.

JULY

IN FAIRLY SHARP CONTRAST to the previous month, July is usually the period when the Troop concentrates on performing the Musical Drive at military tattoos and agricultural shows around the country. Until 1999 the greater part of July was always taken up with the Royal Tournament, held at the Earl's Court Exhibition Centre in London. For 2002, the Troop were involved in the spectacular *Army 2002* display at Larkhill on Salisbury Plain, and later in the month spent a very enjoyable week at the Royal Welsh Show in Builth Wells.

Previous page: The Troop rehearsing at the *Army 2002* Exhibition and Display on Salisbury Plain.

Below: The old meets the new. An intriguing picture of the Troop rehearsing at *Army 2002* within the shadow of the Army's very latest self-propelled howitzers, the AS90.

Right: The victorious ladies' tug-of-war team from the King's Troop at *Army 2002*.
Below: A scene of action and activity as the Troop 'limber-up' and come out of action during one of the many rehearsals at *Army 2002*.

The Parade Commander's trumpeter sounds the order 'Walk, March', as the Troop make their entry into the arena at *Army 2002*.

Speed and drama as the gun-teams gallop out of the arena at *Army 2002*.

Scenes from the Musical
Drive and Display at
the Royal Welsh Show,
Builth Wells.

Opposite, left and right: Behind the scenes at Builth Wells.

Below: Between performing at *Army 2002* and the Royal Welsh, the Troop also spent time at the Sandringham Show. They are shown *en route* to the arena to perform the Musical Drive and Display.

AUGUST

THE MONTH OF AUGUST marks the end of the summer show season and a return to ceremonial duties. In 2002, for the first time in more than fifty years, the customary Royal Salute fired on 4 August for the Queen Mother's birthday was no longer required. Thus, the soldiers of the King's Troop were plunged almost immediately into the business of training for the annual duty of furnishing the Queen's Life Guard at Whitehall.

This duty normally lasts for about three weeks, and allows the Household Cavalry the opportunity to take a well-earned break from ceremonial duties. Whilst Life Guard is taking place some members of the Troop are able to enjoy a brief spell of summer leave. Others are involved with recruiting tours or instructing in the Army Saddle Clubs Association Equitation Course which takes place at St. John's Wood each year.

Previous page: The Orderly Officer inspects the Queen's Life Guard, found by the King's Troop, at the '4 o'clock Parade'.

Left: All three subjects in this photograph of a 'Boxman' on duty at Horse Guards, seem to be enjoying the occasion!

Opposite: The Old Guard passes the Queen Victoria Memorial at the front of Buckingham Palace on its way back to St. John's Wood.

Routine scenes at
St. John's Wood.

Left: A view through the
section lines.

Below: Hosing down.
Opposite: Jumping
practice in the Riding
School.

Left: Students on the Army Saddle Clubs Association Course being put through their paces in the manège.

SEPTEMBER

THE QUEEN'S LIFE GUARD normally comes to an end in the first week of September. After a few days spent placing the harness and guns into a state of light care and preservation, the Troop disperses to various parts of the country for the annual Section and Troop camps. One of the most enjoyable periods of the year for both horses and soldiers, these camps last for about two weeks. Ideally, they are located as near to the coast as possible, with a good beach close at hand. This ensures that morning exercise can include a swim for the horses – something they absolutely adore!

Apart from the fun of swimming with the horses in the sea, there is the serious business of competing for the various mounted sports trophies during the Troop sports day. Among the competitions, which include show-jumping classes at virtually every level in the fiercely fought Recruits Jumping class! In addition, there are traditional gymkhana classes and a peculiarly military competition, the VC Race, which simulates the rescue of a 'wounded' soldier by his mounted comrade.

Previous page: The bronze guardsmen at the front of the Guards War Memorial look on in silent approval as the 'Old Guard' of the King's Troop at the end of their duty at Horse Guards Parade prepare to hand over to the 'New Guard' of the Blues and Royals.

Opposite: The Orderly Officer makes his way through London's busy traffic on his lonely journey to Horse Guards for the daily 4 o'clock inspection.

The 'Arms Guard' salutes as a VIP passes through Horse Guards.

The Orderly Officer inspects the 'Boxmen' at the daily parade at 4 o'clock at Horse Guards.

Opposite, above: In cloak order, the 'New Guard' pass through Hyde Park on their way to Horse Guards Parade.

Opposite: A happy group of local children are introduced to the horses during the Troop's stay at Abbotsham, North Devon.

Above: After the busy life of ceremonial in London the relaxation and fresh air of of the seaside is a welcome change.

Right: Horses and men enjoying the surf and sand at Westward Ho! North Devon.

OCTOBER

WITH BOTH HORSES AND MEN suitably refreshed from the fun and excitement of Troop Camp, the return to St. John's Wood and the hustle and bustle of London brings every-one back to the reality of everyday soldiering. This is the month when the Troop trains its newest members – horses, which are called 'remounts', and soldiers. The remounts are almost all Irish light draught horses and arrive from the Defence Animal Centre at Melton Mowbray in Leicestershire, in the early part of the month. Ordinarily it takes about six weeks to break and train these young horses to the saddle and then they are posted to their sub-sections for further training in draught work. Most of the soldiers will have arrived at the Wood since the beginning of the year. They attend the 'Recruits Rides', whilst other, more experienced, soldiers attend further upgrading courses in the months leading up to Christmas. This month also signals the start of the hunting season and winter training. Everyone in the Troop has the opportunity to hunt; most support the Royal Artillery Hunt on Salisbury Plain, whilst others are fortunate enough to spend time at Melton Mowbray.

Previous page: The Commanding Officer and Adjutant lead the Troop on their way to yet another training session at Wormwood Scrubs.

Above and opposite: An unusual addition to the annual calendar was the provision of Troop personnel to act as fire-fighters. Despite this, much of the life of the Troop continued as before – as can be seen in the background to these photographs.

The armed guard at the guardroom reminds all-comers of the serious side of the Army.

The arrival of the new young horses at Melton Mowbray – known in the Army as 'remounts', requires much patience and a lot of hard work before they will be ready to take their part in State ceremonial.

Troop Equitation Instructor casts an approving eye over the latest 'remounts' in the section lines.

NOVEMBER

As THE INDIVIDUAL TRAINING programme continues, the business of State ceremonial returns during the month with the annual Remembrance Sunday parade and, the following weekend, participation in the Lord Mayor's Show. Depending upon the political calendar there may also be a Royal Salute – the last of the year, to mark the State Opening of Parliament. For the Remembrance Sunday Parade the Troop traditionally provides the minute guns which, fired from Horse Guards Parade, mark the two minutes silence for the Nation. In addition the Troop provides a dismounted detachment to represent the Royal Artillery at the Cenotaph and trumpeters for the Royal Artillery Service of Remembrance at Hyde Park Corner. For the Lord Mayor's Show, two complete sub-sections take part in the procession through the streets of the City of London.

Previous page: The dismounted detachment from the King's Troop arrives at the Cenotaph for the annual Armistice Day parade.

Above: Close-up of the State Trumpeters.

Left: In cloak order, a section from the Kings Troop marches through the streets of the city of London during the annual Lord Mayor's Show.

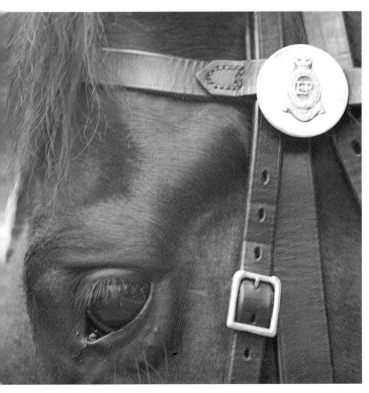

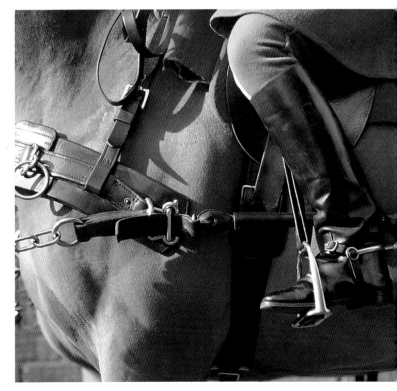

Opposite, left and below left: The Troop formed up on the square at St. John's Wood (minus detachments) before moving off to Hyde Park to fire a 41-gun salute marking the State Opening of Parliament.

Below: The Troop in Hyde Park *en route* to Buckingham Palace.

Opposite, above: The Salute in progress.
Opposite, below: Riding in the Irish State Coach, Her Majesty The Queen returns to Buckingham Palace from the ceremonial State Opening of Parliament at the Palace of Westminster.

Above: The Troop march past Her Majesty The Queen in the quadrangle at Buckingham Palace at the conclusion of the Royal Salute.

The Troop officers, and companions, at the end of a long day.

DECEMBER

DECEMBER IS THE MONTH when the remounts return to St. John's Wood; the individual course programme is completed; and the hard work of those involved is rewarded when they 'pass out', trained and qualified to ride on parade. It is also the festive season and by the middle of the month the first half of the Troop disappear for a well earned few weeks leave with their families. Before this, however, there is normally a special Troop show-jumping competition which, in keeping with the season, is performed in fancy dress. For those on duty over the Christmas period there are the usual festivities and celebrations to enjoy, including the annual tour of St. John's Wood to spread a little seasonal good cheer among the local inhabitants. On Christmas Day the soldiers are treated to a late start as the officers and SNCOs carry out the traditional task of mucking out the horses. This is usually followed by a hearty breakfast in the sergeants' mess and at lunchtime everyone gathers in the soldiers' dining hall for the serving of Christmas Dinner. The horses, too, are treated to some special tit-bits on this day, normally provided by the soldiers themselves.

Previous page: Driver training at Wormwood Scrubs.

Below: A detachment ride in the manège.

Harness cleaning, traditionally known as 'rifting'.

Below (left and right): A farrier at work, and the saddler's workbench.

Below: The Troop led by a carriage go on their Christmas rounds in St. John's Wood.

Local residents greet the Troop with handshakes and mince pies during their Christmas tour.

The officers of the Troop relax in the comfortable surroundings of the Officers' Mess.

Commanding Officers, The King's Troop Royal Horse Artillery

Acknowledgements

It has been almost 20 years since Malcolm Wallace produced his excellent book *The King's Troop Royal Horse Artillery*. It is perhaps timely, therefore, that in a period when change has been the only constant, that a new, up-to-date record of the Troop should be published. Many people have contributed to its preparation. In particular we would like to mention Barbara Cooper, for editing and supervising the production of the book; Major Bill Clarke, for writing the text and captions and working closely with the designer; His Grace the Duke of Richmond, for writing the Foreword; and Major-General Sir Evelyn Webb-Carter to whose initial idea and encouragement we owe the book's publication.

This book has been produced with financial help from:
Alenia Marconi Systems
Mr Stephen Moriarty QC
Mr & Mrs R D Southern

Bibliography

Bidewell, Brigadier Shelford *The Royal Horse Artillery*
Clarke, Major W. G *Horse Gunners – 200 years of Panache & Professionalism*
Probert, Lieutenant Colonel RHC *Some Brief Reference Notes on the Royal Horse Artillery*
Wallace, Major M. C. R. *The King's Troop Royal Horse Artillery*
Wanklyn, Joan *Guns at the Wood*

Opposite: The Ceremony of Retreat, lowering the flag at 1800hrs.

Index

PICTURE CREDITS

Julian Calder
Cover. Pages 1, 8, 32, 36, 38, 44, 46, 47, 50, 58/59, 61, 62, 63, 70, 71, 75, 76, 78/79, 80, 81, 82, 83, 84, 85, 86/87, 90, 91, 94, 95, 96, 97, 98/99, 100, 101, 102, 103, 106, 107, 111, 112/113, 114, 115, 116, 117 & 118.

Henry Dallal
Pages 2/3, 30/31, 33, 34, 35, 36, 37, 38, 39, 40, 41/42, 43, 44, 45, 50, 51, 52, 53, 55, 56, 57, 60, 64, 65/66, 67, 68, 69, 72/73, 74, 76, 77, 88, 89, 92/93, 104/105, 106, 107, 108, 109, 110 & 111.

Bombardier Darren Gray
Pages 48, 49, 54, 55, 57 to 60.

Sergeant Sean Lewis
Page 29.

Hugh Evelyn Prints
Page 6.

The Imperial War Museum
Pages 13, 14, 15, 16, 17 & 18.

The Royal Artillery Institution
Pages 10, 12, 13 & 14.

In spite of careful research, including that through the Design and Artists Copyright Society, it has not been possible to trace the original owners or copyright holders of the photographs on pages 20 to 27.

Printed by Eurolitho S.p.A., Italy.